Computer Operating Systems
Beginner's Practical Guide

Dr. Mohammed Fakrudeen

Associate Lecturer & Researcher
Anglia Ruskin University, Chelmsford
United Kingdom.

Dr. Shahanawaj Ahamad

Assistant Professor
College of Computer Science &
Engineering, University of Hail
Hail, Saudi Arabia.

July, 2017

Computer Operating Systems
Beginner's Practical Guide

ISBN-10: 1548735477

ISBN-13: 978-1-5487354-7-0

Preface

This practical guide is designed and compiled for the early stage students, learning basics of operating systems and applying commands in lab exercises. It contents the important contents about the practical aspects such as objectives and outcomes of the studies, implementation policies of the lab exercises, and instructions for the experiments. It also guides the lab scheduling and work flows. Each individual lab unit consists of lab objectives, background, and assignments. This book will be an effective guide to accomplish the lab experiments for undergraduate college students.

Mohammed Fakrudeen & Shahanawaj Ahamad

July, 2017

Contents

General Information

Title: **Computer Operating Systems Beginner's Practical Guide**

DESCRIPTION

GENERAL COMPETENCE FOR LAB: Developing an understanding and competent use of a Multi User Operating System.

LEARNING OUTCOMES

1.   Describe the characteristics of a multi user operating system;

2.   Manipulate files and directories;

3.   Use the facilities of a multi user operating system.

Learning Objectives

LEARNING OUTCOME

1.   DESCRIBE THE CHARACTERISTICS OF A MULTI USER OPERATING SYSTEM

PERFORMANCE CRITERIA

(a)   Describe the principal features of a multi user operating system.

(b)   Distinguish types of multi user operating system.

(c)   Outline the main physical components of a multi user computer system.

(d)   List the principal components of multi user operating system software.

RANGE STATEMENT

Features: resource sharing; multi-tasking; background processing.

Types: multi-processor; time-slice; distributed.

Physical components: processors; memory; data storage devices; terminals; output devices.

Software components: kernel; device handlers; spoolers; use interface.

LEARNING OUTCOME

2.   MANIPULATE FILES AND DIRECTORIES

PERFORMANCE CRITERIA

(a)   File and directory commands are used correctly.

(b)   File and directory naming conforms to organizational standards.

(c)   System editor is used to create and amend text files.

(d)   File and directory access rights are determined and altered.

(e)   Print system is correctly used.

RANGE STATEMENT

Commands: file and directory creation; moving; listing and deletion; directory change.

Editor: file saving and loading; character insertion and deletion; block move, copy and delete;

search and replace.

Access rights: read/write; user; group.

Print system: submit; check status; cancel; select printer.

LEARNING OUTCOME

3. USE THE FACILITIES OF A MULTI USER OPERATING SYSTEM

PERFORMANCE CRITERIA

(a) User connection facilities are used correctly.

(b) Common commands and command switches are used correctly.

(c) Main system is used correctly.

(d) User environment is configured to meet requirements.

(e) Input/output redirection facilities are correctly used.

RANGE STATEMENT

User connection facilities: login; logout; virtual screens; terminal type.

Commands: help system; device related; process control; file locate.

Mail: single address; multiple addresses.

Redirection facilities: redirectors; pipes; filters.

Unit 1

Understanding the Windows Environment

Exercise – 1

Identify the items and write about it in 2 or 3 lines

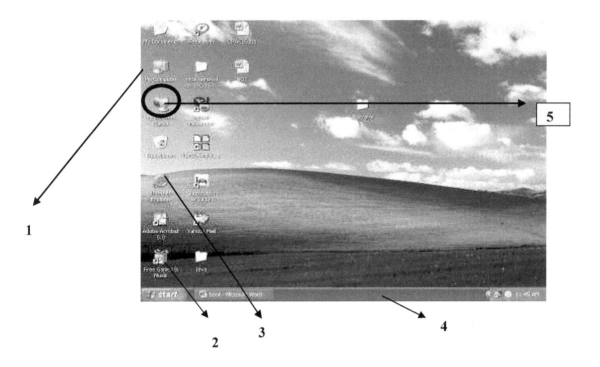

_____ 1.   My computer _____

_____

_____ 2.   Icons _____

_____

_____ 3.   Browser _____

_____

_____ 4.   Taskbar _____

_____

_____ 5.   Network Neighborhood _____

2. Identify the elements in the Windows

Anatomy of a Window

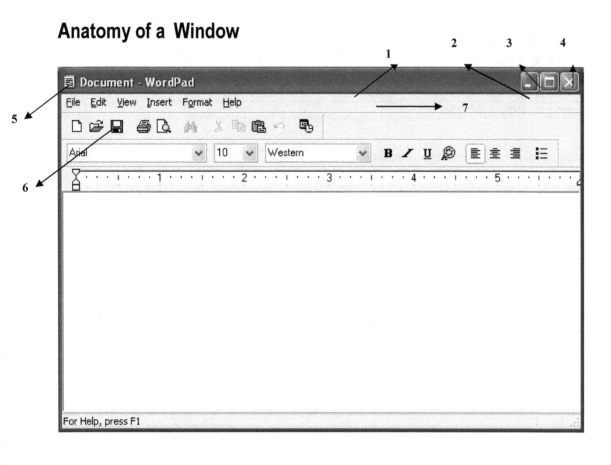

1. _____

2. _____

3. _____

4. _____

5. _____

6. _____

7. _____

3. Write the commands for searching:

1. To search all files	*.*
2. To search all document files	
3. To search for excel file which ends with letter 'd'	
4. To search for all files and folders with 'xyz' in name	
5. To search for folder named 'syscoms'	
6. To search for executable file starting with 'abc'	

4. Find the answer for the following calculation by using calculator:

1. 3*5*2	
2. (25-2) + (15*10) - Use Memory technique	
3. Binary Equivalent of 56	
4. 8^3	
5. 19^2 – Don't type 19 two times	
6. 12^9	
7. $2 * pi * 5^2$	
8. NOT 7	
9. 5 XOR 2	
10. Tan 30 in Radians	

Exercise 2

Create the following directory structure by using MS DOS Commands. (The contents of the text files follow the directory structure.)

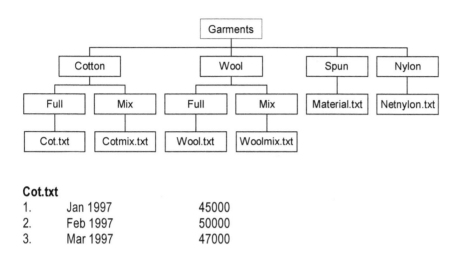

Cot.txt

1.	Jan 1997	45000
2.	Feb 1997	50000
3.	Mar 1997	47000

Cotmix.txt

1.	Jan 1997	45000
2.	Feb 1997	50000
3.	Mar 1997	47500

Wool.txt

The sale of wool in the year 1997 was 19,000,000, which was much higher that the sale of the previous year.

Woolmix.txt

The word woolmix stands for a product that is a mixture of wool with polyester. The ratio of the mixture is 3:2.

Material.txt

This includes all materials including cotton, silk, polyester, wool, dacron, terry-cotton etc.

Netnylon.txt

Netnylon has become very popular due to its durability and toughness. More and more people are opting to it. Consequently the price of the material is dropping.

Perform the following using DOS Commands:

1. After you finish creating the directory structure write the path of "Wool.txt" file by using windows Explorer.
2. Delete the directory "Nylon".
3. Copy the files "Cot.txt" and "Cotmix.txt" to the "Spun" directory.
4. Rename the file "Cot.txt" to "Cotton.txt"
5. Move the file "materials.txt" to the "Garments" directory

Unit 2

Understanding the Windows Utilities

Exercise 3

1. Draw a picture in MS Paint and save it as "uoh.bmp"
2. By using Display option in the control panel change the wallpaper of desktop to "uoh.bmp" and image should be stretched.
3. If you're a left handed person, change the button position of the mouse
4. if you're a right handed person, revert back the mouse settings
5. Set the screen resolution to 1280 by 720 pixels
6. Type "USA" in screen saver with the font style as : Verdana, Bold, 48 and in random position
7. Add "Command Prompt" in schedule task and set schedule task at system startup and use the option not to run this task if it is running in batteries [Accessories |system tools|backup]
8. Change the currency to "USD"
9. Find out the following information about your computer and note it down as shown below:

Computer Name _____

Capacity of RAM _____

Operating System _____

Type of Processor _____

Exercise 4

1. If anti-virus is installed , scan the "Garment " folder which you created in previous exercises
2. Set the scanning should be started automatically 2 days in a week from 10 am onwards
3. If any virus is detected, write the name of the virus below:

_____

_____

_____

_____

_____

Exercise 5

1. Take the backup of "Garments" folder [Accessories |system tools|backup]
2. Schedule the backup if needed
3. What is the backup media (CD or magnetic tape or external hard disk) used? Why?

_____

_____

_____

_____

_____

_____

4. Did you took normal backup or incremental backup? Why?

_____

_____

_____

_____

5. What is the difference between disk clean up and disk defragmentation[Accessories |system tools]

6. How will you install the printer and what is the ipaddress of the printer? What is the purpose of the driver software?

7. IF you press any key in the keyboard, how OS will identify that key has been pressed?. Find different IRQ for the peripheral device in the Windows.

8. What type of security is present in the windows? [Type "Demo: Security basics" in the help and watch the video]

Unit 3

Understanding the architecture of Multi user Operating System (UNIX)

Objectives

1. Definition of MUOS
2. Architecture of Operating System
3. Peer-to-peer Network
4. Resource Sharing
5. Multitasking
6. Processing
   a. Foreground Processing
   b. Background Processing
7. Swapping
8. Paging
9. Types of MUOS
10. Multiprocessor
11. Time-Slice
    a. Distributed
    b. Hardware Components
    c. Processor
    d. Memory
    e. Storage Devices
12. Terminals
    a. Output Devices
    b. Terminal Connectivity
    c. Telnet Protocols

Notes

1. Definition of MUOS
   a. An operating system is a software program that acts as an intermediate linking a user of the computer and the computer hardware.
   b. It will provide the user with a flexible and manageable means of control over the resources of the computer

2. Architecture of Operating System

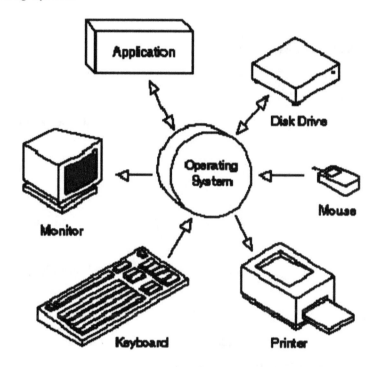

3. Peer-to-peer Network
   a. Networks can allow computers, servers, and other devices to talk to each other.
   b. If you only need to share a printer or an Internet connection we can select workgroup network.

4. Resource Sharing
   a. Resource sharing takes place when all the terminals connected to a server can use the peripheral devices attached to the server without having a direct connection to any of these devices

5. Multi-Tasking
   a. An Operating systems that is capable of allowing multiple software processes to be run at the same time.
   b. eg.
      i. Unix

      ii.   Linux

      iii.   Windows 2000

      iv.   Windows 2003

6. Processing

   a. The process manager manages the scheduling of processes. A process is an open application. The number of processes is limited only by available memory.

   b. There are mainly two types of processing are there.

      i.   Foreground Process.

      ii.   Background Process.

7. Processing

   a. Background Processing

      i. Processing in which the program is not visibly interacting with the user.

   b. Foreground Processing

      i. Process in which currently interacting with user it appears to the user as an active application.

8. Swapping

   a. To replace pages or segment of data in memory. Swapping is a useful technique that enables a computer to execute programs and manipulate data files larger than main memory.

   b. DOS does not perform swapping, but most other operating systems including Windows & UNIX do.

9. Paging

   a. A technique used by virtual memory operating system to help ensures that the data you need is available as quickly as possible.

10. Types of MUOS

   a. A multi-user operating system allows many different users to take advantage of the computer's resources simultaneously. There are various types of Multi User Operating Systems are available.

      i.   Unix / Linux

      ii.   Main Frame operating System

      iii. Windows 2000

      iv. Novell Netware

11. Multiprocessor

   a. Multiprocessor systems have more than one processor in close communication sharing the computer bus, the clock and sometime memory and peripheral devices.

12. Time-Slice

   a. In a time sharing system time-slice is given to each of the processes for execution. In order to prevent a user program from getting stuck in an infinite loop and never returning control to the operating system we can use a timer

13. Distributed

   a. In the distributed system's processors do not share memories or a clock; instead each of the processors has a local memory. The processors communicate with each other with the help of high-speed buses or telephone lines.

14. Hardware Components

   a. Components which required running your computers.

      i.   Processor
      ii.   Memory
      iii. Storage Devices
      iv.   Terminals
      v.   Output Devices

15. Processor

   a. It plays a vital role in the realization of the features of the Multi-user operating system. Since it is multi-user operating system which support multi-processing the processor must possess high clock speed.

16. Memory

   a. In a multi user operating system, the memory size should be quiet high. There are many users accessing data from the server at the same time, the ram size should be as high as possible

17. Storage Devices

   a. The hard disk or the floppy disk etc. is the storage devices which are shared by all the users. The users at the terminals save their files at their users directory, which is saved in the hard disk, located at the server.

18. Terminals

   a. Terminal login privileges and connect-time are controlled using only user attributes to implement a renewable resource model, with hierarchical limits. The kernel is not directly involved, other than providing a simple facility for helping identify exactly when a user logs in and out.

19. Output Devices

   a. The output devices are the peripherals connected to the server. The monitor is an input/output device, which enables the user to send as well as receive data. Another output device is the printer, which is connected to the server and can be accessed by all the terminals connected to the server. The printer is used to print files. The users give the print command to print a particular file at their terminals. This print request is sent to the printer buffer and lies in queue to be printed.

20. Terminal Connectivity

    a. The invention provides a new and improved system for transferring information between a host system and a terminal system. It also provides user to connect server and access multiple shared resources with the help of different protocols.

21. Telnet Protocols

    a. Two Transmission Control Protocol/Internet Protocols (TCP/IP), Telnet and rlogin, enable connections to a host.

    b. Telnet, a virtual terminal protocol that is part of the TCP/IP protocol suite, is most widely used protocol.

Software Components of UNIX

Objectives

1. Software Components

    a. A user uses the command line to send commands to the shell. The shell translates those commands into kernel speak. And finally, the kernel sends them on to the hardware. The image below shows this relationship.

        i. Kernel / Shell

        ii. Device Handlers

        iii. Device File

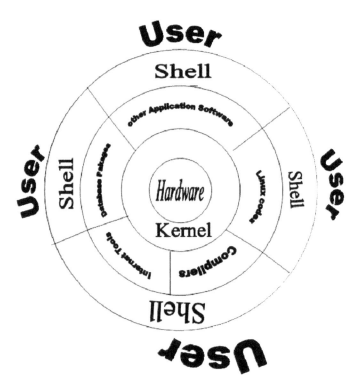

2. Kernel

    a. The kernel is responsible for low level   hardware communication.

    b. Kernel manages the machine's hardware resources (including the processor and the memory), and provides and controls the way any other software component can access these resources.

3. Shell

    a. The shell provides human users with a user-friendly interface.

    b. The shell is a command interpreter, it interprets the commands given by the user and puts it in to action

4. Device Handlers

    a. Device handlers are also known as device drivers. In this the device handlers have device files used to manage and utilize the drivers properly.

    b. In this it handles the devices connected to the server, which are used by the users at different terminals.

5. Spoolers

    a. Spooling refers to putting jobs in a buffer.

    b. Spoolers are where data is stored prior to it being processed. They behave like temporary storage devices.

6. User Interface

    a. An operating system provides a way for users to run programs and access the file system.

    b. Linux has both graphical and text-based user interfaces. GNOME and KDE provide graphical user interfaces.

7. Unix Operating System

    a. UNIX is a computer Operating System originally developed in the 1960s and 1970s by a group of AT &T Bell Labs employees including Ken Thompson, Dennis Ritchie, and Douglas McIlroy.

    b. UNIX was designed to be Portable, Multi-Tasking and Multi-User.

8. Unix File System

    a. Every item in a UNIX file system can be defined as belonging to one of four possible types

        i. Ordinary files

        ii. Directories

        iii. Device files

        iv. Links

9. Ordinary Files

    a. Ordinary files can contain text, data, or program information. An ordinary file cannot contain another file, or directory.

10. Directories
    a. Directories can containers that can hold files, and other directories. A directory is actually implemented as a file that has one line for each item contained within the directory.

11. Device Files
    a. Device files represent input/output (i/o) devices, like a tty (terminal), a disk drive, or a printer.
    b. Device files can be either *character special files,* that deal with streams of characters, or *block special files*, that operate on larger blocks of data

12. Structure for File System

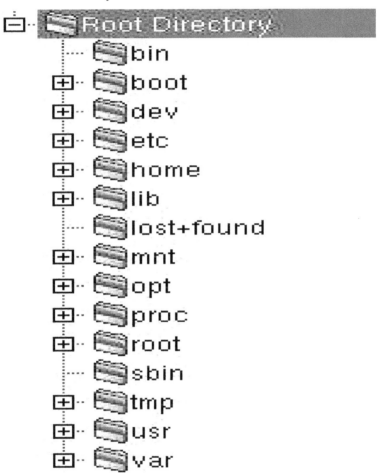

Root Directory:

This is a mandatory directory. It is the beginning of the file system and includes all of the directories beneath it.

/bin:

This is a mandatory directory. This directory contains the **bin**aries that are used in single-user systems. For multi-user systems these binaries are usually stored in the /usr/bin directory.

/boot:

This is a mandatory directory. This directory stores the files which are used for the system startup except for the configuration and the map installer. Frequently the kernel is stored here especially if more than one kernel is installed.

/dev:

This is a mandatory directory. The device files, sockets, and named pipes are stored here.

/etc:

This is a mandatory directory. This directory, pronounced "et-see", holds the configuration files for the system.

/home:

This is an optional but widely used directory. The other variation on the /home directory is to use a subdirectory in the /var directory. This is where users will do most of their work. Each user is given their own directory in the /home directory which is theirs to organize and use as they choose.

/lib:

This is a mandatory directory. Shared libraries needed at bootup or which need to be run by top level commands is stored here.

/mnt:

This is an optional but very popular directory. This directory contains mount points for external storage devices. To access a floppy disk drive you cd to mnt/floppy. Once an external drive is accessed, its file system is mounted to the host system in the /mnt directory.

/opt:

This is an optional directory. It is a directory intended to contain software packages which are added to the original system. On my system it is present, but empty.

/proc:

This is an optional but widely used directory. It contains a virtual file system which is created and used by the currently running kernel. It is deleted when the system is shut down. Frequently, monitoring programs use the /proc directory to obtain information on currently running processes and other environmental information.

/root:

This is an optional but widely used directory. It is often created to eliminate clutter from the "/" directory. It contains configuration files for the root user.

/sbin:

This is a mandatory directory. This directory was originally a place to store static binaries. It has been expanded to include administrative binaries which are used by the root user only.

Unit 4

File Commands

File Commands

1. Login Procedure
    a. Connect to the server by using Telnet service, and Specify user Name & Password.

2. Shutdown Procedure
    a. Turn off the computer immediately or at a specified time.
    b. SYNTAX
        i. *shutdown [-a][-t sec] [time] [warning-message]*

3. Login Details
    a. Linux maintain an account of all the current users of the system.
    b. Command:
        i. $ W
        ii. $ Who

4. Changing the Password
    a. In Linux if you want to change password you can change your password by specifying old password.
    b. Command: $ passwd

5. Checking Current Directory
    a. It is a remarkable future of the Linux system that, like a file, a user also copies a certain slot in the file system.
    b. Command:
        i. $ pwd

6. Clearing the Screen
    a. In Linux if you want to clear the terminal screen use Clear Command.
    b. Command:
        i. $ clear

7. Creating a File
    a. cat is useful for creating a file. In order to create small files, Enter the command cat followed by the > (the right chevron) character and the file name.
    b. Command:
        i. $ cat> hello
        ii. where hello is the file name

8. Displaying Content of a File

    a. cat is one of the most well-known command of Linux system. It mainly used to display the content of a small file on the terminal.

    b. Command:

        i. $ cat *filename*

9. Making a Directory

    a. Like in Dos, directories can be created with the mkdir (make directory) command. The command is followed by the names of the directories to be created.

    b. Command:

        i. $ mkdir *dir1 dir2 dir3*

10. Listing Directories

    a. This command will obtain a list of all files in the current directory.

    b. Command:

        i. $ ls

    c. Options:

        i.   -x
        ii.   -F
        iii. -r
        iv.   -a
        v.   -R
        vi.   -l
        vii. -d
        viii. -t
        ix.   -u
        x.   -l

11. Changing Directories

    a. You can move around in the file system by using the cd (change directory) command. It changes the current directory to the directory specified as the argument.

    b. Command:

        i. $ pwd

        ii. $ cd directory name

12. Removing Directory

    a. Like in Dos, directories can be removed by using rmdir (remove directory) command. The command is followed by the names of the directories to be removed.

    b. Command:

        i. $ rmdir [options] *Dirctoy Name*

        ii. *Options : -f, -l, -r*

13. Copying a File

    a. The cp (copy) command copies a file or a group of files.

    b. Command:

        i. $ cp (source file) (destination file)

14. Linking a File

    a. The ln (link) command copies a file or a group of files to destination file and if you change anything in source file, it will update automatically in source file.

    b. Command:

        i. $ cp (source file) (destination file)

15. Renaming a File

    a. You can use move command to rename files or directories.

    b. Command:

    c. $ mv file1 file2   Where: file1 is old file name file2 is new file name

16. Comparing Two Files

    a. The command which use to compare two files.

    b. Command:

        i. $ cmp [file name] [file name]

Exercise

Create the following directory structure. (The contents of the text files follow the directory structure.)

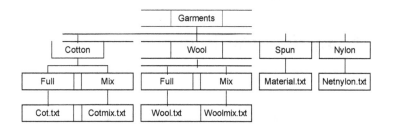

Cot.txt

1.	Jan 1997	45000
2.	Feb 1997	50000
3.	Mar 1997	47000

Cotmix.txt

1.	Jan 1997	45000
2.	Feb 1997	50000
3.	Mar 1997	47500

Wool.txt
The sale of wool in the year 1997 was 19,000,000, which was much higher that the sale of the previous year.

Woolmix.txt
The word woolmix stands for a product that is a mixture of wool with polyester. The ratio of the mixture is 3:2.

Material.txt
This includes all materials including cotton, silk, polyester, wool, dacron, terry-cotton etc.

Netnylon.txt
Netnylon has become very popular due to its durability and toughness. More and more people are opting to it. Consequently the price of the material is dropping.

[1] Make a copy of the file Cotmix.txt into another file Cotmix1.txt

[2] Create a file matter and type any two sentences in it.

[3] Combine the contents of the file Cotmix.txt and matter into another file txtmat.

[4] Delete the file Cotmix1.txt.

[5] Create one more link called tmpfile for the file matter

[6] Rename the file Cotmix to Cottonmix.

[7] Create another directory newdir within the directory Spun.

[8] Copy the contents of Nylon directory to the newdir directory.

[9] Delete the directories mydir and newdir and their contents at one shot.

[10] Check the path to the current directory.

Unit 5

Analyzing the Files

The main features of a multi-user operating system are as follows:

(a)   resource-sharing

(b)   multitasking

(c)   background processing.

Each feature is explained below in detail:

(a)   Resource-sharing:

Resource sharing takes place when all the terminals connected to a server can use the peripheral devices attached to the server without having a direct connection to any of these devices. In a multi-user operating system, there will normally be an option that allows client computers to use a printer or scanner that is connected to the server machine.

Data can also be shared between two or computers by enabling a particular file or document's 'Sharing' attribute. Word documents, Excel Worksheets, Bitmap images and various other types of data can be shared between systems, as long as the client computer supports the software being used.

When we say resource sharing, we mean sharing one or two printers or scanners or any peripheral hardware devices for a multiple number of computer systems.
The advantage of resource sharing is that it reduces expenses because in such a case, there is no need to purchase printers or scanners for each terminal in the network.

(b)   Multitasking:

A multitasking operating system is a system that allows the CPU to execute multiple jobs (more than one task) at the same time by switching or swapping between them. Every command we give to the computer is called a task. These switches happen so frequently that the user can interact with each program while they are running. During multitasking, several programs reside together in the RAM and are executed simultaneously.

With multitasking, we can save a lot of time as we have all the applications available on a single platform and need not spend time in opening and closing the applications. Although the applications appear to be running simultaneously, in reality each program runs for a short period of time in turn, one after another. So, the processing is not actually simultaneous. But, the switching of programs happens so quickly it appears to be simultaneous.

As a result, we could be sorting a database and calculating a spreadsheet while we are writing a letter on notepad or even working on some other task at the same time. To work with different applications at the same time, we would have to switch between the applications often, generally using the taskbar.

Another example of multitasking is when the computer might be printing out a data file, while at the same time the user is running a word processing program to enter a document.

Operating systems that allow multiple software processes to be run at the same time are said to be multi-tasking. In such cases, the multi-tasking CPU divides its ability to satisfy the demands of different components in the computer at the same time.

Operating systems that would fall into this category are:

UNIX

Windows 2000

A multi-tasking operating system can also be called as a Time-shared operating system when a number of computers are networked with each other. Such a system uses CPU scheduling and multiprogramming to provide each user with a small portion of memory from the server computer. Whenever a user from a client computer logs in to the network a small memory space is allocated to the user. This is why the user feels that he is working on a single standalone system, rather than on a network.

(c)   Background processing:

If a user can run more than one process at the any instant on a particular operating system, then that operating system is said to support multi-tasking. Apart from a single multi process in the foreground, the user can run more than one program in the background without the processes interfering with each other. This is called background processing.

Foreground and background processes have different response-time requirements, and so might have different scheduling needs. In addition, foreground processes may have priority (externally defined) over background processes.

An example for background processing is playing music in the background while working on a word processor at the same time.

1. The Calendar
    a. With the command you can display the calendar for the period of one year or for particular month of the year.
    b. Command:

       i. $ cal *[Year]*

      ii. $cal month year

     iii. $ cal year|more

2. Display the System Date

   a. This command will display the current date of system.

   b. Command.

       i. $ date

      ii. $ date+%m

     iii. $ date+%h

     iv. $ date +"%h %m"

   c. Try with other options like d, y, H, M and S

3. On-Line Help

   a. Command used to display the online help facility.

   b. Command:

       i. $ man[command]

   c. To display the compact listing of all the option.

   d. Command:

       i. $ *Command*--help

4. Details of Users

   a. command which is having communicative feature, it simply produces a list of all logged users.

   b. Command:

       i. $ finger

      ii. $finger username

5. To find the id of the user

   a. Type the command,

       i. $id

6. To Display Message

   a. To display any message

       i. $echo message

   b. For Example,

       i. $echo "Welcome 2 all"

7. calculator

    a. $ bc

       2+3

       5

       2*5;2^8

       10

       256

       13/2

       6

       scale=2 13/2

       6.50

8. Pattern Matching (Wild card patterns)

    a. The shell enables specification of a general pattern of characters in the command line to match a group of file names.

    b. Options:

       i. ? (single character)

       ii. * (many characters)

9. Line, Word & Character Counting

    a. The command is used to count the line, word & characters from the specified files.

    b. Command:

       i. *$ wc [options] {file Name}*

    c. Options:

       i. -c

       ii. -m

       iii. -l

10. Head and Tail

    a. To display first four lines of red file

       i. $head -4 red

    b. To display last 3 lines of good file

       i. $tail -3 good

    c. To display from 2nd line

       i. $tail +2 red

11. Input- Output Redirection

    a. Output Redirection(>)

       i. $date>today

      ii. $cat today

  b. Input Redirection(<)

      i. $cat<today

  c. Input-output Redirection

      i. $cat<today>red

Exercise 4

Perform the above the command first and then answer the following questions

[1] Find out who are the other users logged on to the unix environment and save this information in a text file.

[2] Find which day it is [should display only the day and not whole date] [3] View the first 2 lines of the text file Cot.txt

[4] View the last line of the text file Cot.txt.

[5] List the current directory.

[6] Count the number of words the text file 'Cot.txt is made up of.

[7] How many words are present in Wool.txt

[8] Display from the 2nd line of Cot.txt

[9] Using input-output redirection, create a copy of Wool.txt to Woll1.txt

Unit 6

File Operations and File Security

The three main types of multi-user operating systems are as follows:

1) Multiprocessor Systems.

Multiprocessor systems are those systems that have multiple processors, i.e. two, three or even up to ten central processing units attached to them.

Such systems have a large memory bank or a high storage capacity.

Even if one processor fails, or is too busy, another processor can take over functioning. Therefore, at any given time, no processor can remain completely idle. Such systems also increase reliability. If functions can be distributed properly among several processors, then the failure of one processor will not halt the system, but will rather only slow it down. This ability to continue providing service proportional to the level of no failed hardware is called graceful degradation.

Multiprocessors can also save money compared to several single systems because the processor can share peripherals, cabinets and power supplies.

Systems that have more than one processor in close communication, sharing the computer bus, the clock, and sometimes memory and peripheral devices are called tightly coupled systems.

The basic advantages of a multiprocessor system can therefore be summarized as follows:

1) Fault tolerant. There is very little scope for any kinds of errors or faults because of the multiple numbers of processors in operation.
2) Graceful degradation.
3) Reliability.
4) Economical, in some cases.

A multiprocessor consists of two or more processors in a system. In addition to this, a multiprocessor system may have other shared resources. For example, a printer may be connected or available to all CPUs.

To prevent conflicting use of shared resources by several processors, there must be a provision for assigning resources to processors. This task is given to the operating system.

The organization commonly used in the design of operating systems for multiprocessors is the master-slave configuration.

In a master-slave mode (asymmetric multiprogramming), one processor, designated the master, always executes the operating system functions. The remaining processors, denoted as slaves do not perform operating system functions unless it requests by interrupting the master processor. The disadvantage of this system is that if the master processor fails, the complete processing will halt.

31

In another operating system organization (symmetric multiprogramming), both or all processors have the same equal rights and functions. This organization is more suitable for loosely coupled systems where every processor may have its own copy of the entire operating system.

Synchronization of processes allow for the updating of files.

2) Distributed Systems.

In contrast to tightly coupled microprocessor systems, a distributed system is a collection of processors that that do not share memory or the system clock. Each processor in distributed system has its own local memory. The processors communicate with one another through various communication lines, such as high-speed buses or telephone lines. Thus, these systems are also referred to as loosely coupled systems.

Distributed systems provide the user with access to the various resources that the system maintains. Access to a shared peripheral device or any other resource allows computation speedup and improved data availability, as well as reliability.

Such a system also provides the user with a distributed file system. (A file system is a file-service system whose users, servers and storage devices are dispersed among the various sites of a distributed system).

The processors in a distributed system may vary in size and function. They may include small microprocessors, workstations, minicomputers, and large general-purpose computer systems. These processors are referred to as sites, nodes, and computers and so on, depending on the context in which they are mentioned.

A distributed system must provide various mechanisms for process synchronization and communication, for dealing with the deadlock problem and the variety of failures that are not encountered in a centralized system.

A network, either LAN (local area network), WAN (wide area network) or MAN (metropolitan area network) may be a distributed system. Here, the entire work or job in a large project is divided among all the terminals connected in a network.

The main features of a distributed system are:

Resource sharing. In the case of distributed systems, the different terminals on the network domain share one or two peripheral hardware devices to save costs. The networked computers may share either a common printer or a scanner or any other device that is used by all users but, only for a short while. They may also share data like files, etc.

In general, resource sharing in a distributed system provides mechanisms for sharing files at remote sites, using remote specialized hardware devices (such as high-speed array processor), and performing other operations.

Computation speed: The work is spread across many users in a distributed system, enabling it to be finished at a shorter time span. Thus, a particular computation can be divided into a number of sub computations that can be run concurrently (at the same time), giving the users the advantage of high computation speed.

In addition, if a particular site is currently overloaded with jobs, some of them may be moved to lightly loaded sites. This movement of jobs is called load sharing.

Reliability. If one computer fails in a distributed system, the remaining computers can potentially continue operating. If the system is composed of a number of large general-purpose computers, the failure of one of them will not affect the others. However, if the distributed system consists of many small machines, where each machine is responsible for some crucial system function, then a single failure may effectively halt the operation of the whole system.

Therefore, we can consider distributed systems to be reasonably reliable.

Communication. Computers in a distributed system may are connected to each other using a communication network, which may be digital lines, telephone modems or cable media to enable the exchange of information between different systems. Users may initiate file transfers or communicate with one another via electronic mail.

Windows systems also allow users to frequently share data or transfer data between displays.

3).   Real Time Operating Systems.

Real time operating systems are used in advanced areas where the time factor plays a crucial role in operations. There are rigid time requirements on the operation of a processor or the flow of data, so the Real Time system is often used as a control device in a dedicated application.

Sensors bring data to the computer, which analyzes the data and possibly adjusts controls to modify the sensor inputs. This information about change in conditions helps to avoid unnecessary loss of equipment and fatal accidents.

Systems that control scientific experiments, medical imaging systems, industrial control systems, automobile-engine fuel-injection systems, home appliance controllers, weapons and some display systems are Real Time Operating Systems. A real time OS has well-defined fixed time constraints. The processing must be done within the defined constraints or the system will fail.

File Operations

1. Cut Command

a. Use to cut the fields

b. If delimiter is other than space, use '-d' option

c. To cut the second field

    i. cat>mast

       red   yellow green

       blue   black orange

       purple violet indigo

    ii. $ cat mast

       red   yellow green

       blue   black orange

       purple violet indigo

    iii. $ cut -f2 mast

       yellow

       black

       Violet

d. To cut the second filed if delimter is ':'

    i. $ cat>trans

       hai:good:bad

       welcome:to:syscoms

    ii. $ cat trans

       hai:good:bad

       welcome:to:syscoms

    iii. $ cut -d":" -f2 trans

       good

       to

2. Paste Command

a. It is used to paste the content of the files

    i. $ cat data

       india 200   asia

       china 500   Asia

       nigeria 750   Africa

       maxiew 750   north america

       france 800   europe

    ii. $ cat mast

       red   yellow green

       blue   black orange

       purple violet indigo

    iii. $ paste data mast

```
india   200   asia   red    yellow green
china   500   Asia   blue   black  orange
nigeria 750   Africa purple violet indigo
maxiew  750      north america
france  800      europe
```

3. Tee Command
    a. Used to store the output temporarily
    b. For example
        i. $ cat trans|sort|tee temp|cut -d":" -f1
           hai
           welcome
        ii. $ cat temp
            hai:good:bad
            welcome:to:syscoms

4. Translate Command
    a. Used to translate characters from one to other
    b. For example,
        i. To Convert a file into upper case,
        ii. $ cat data|tr "[a-z]" "[A-Z]"
            INDIA   200   ASIA
            CHINA   500   ASIA
            NIGERIA 750   AFRICA
            MAXIEW 750   NORTH AMERICA
            FRANCE 800   EUROPE

File Permissions

There are two types of security is available
    a. System Level Security.
    b. File Level Security.

1. System Level Security
   A security to enter into Unix or Linux system
   For Example, To Change Password
   Command used to change the password.
                    $ passwd

2. Types of Users

35

a. Owners.

b. Groups.

c. Others.

3. File Permission

a. Read (r)

b. Write (w)

c. Execute(x)

d. Denied(-)

4. Commands for Assigning Permissions

a. ls   : To list the file

b. chmod: To change the mode.

c. chown : To change the ownership.

d. chgrp : To change the group.

5. File Level Security

A settings which you can apply for files or directories. The command to check the permissions of current files & directories.

Command:

$ ls -l (File OR
        DirectoryName) OR
$ ls –la (File OR
DirectoryName

6. Understanding the Permissions

D	r	w	x	r	w	x	r	w	x
	Owner			Group			Others		
Directory	Read	Write	Execute	Read	Write	Execute	Read	Write	**Execute**

7. File Level Security

a. Absolute Mode

The most commonly used syntax for setting for changing the permissions.

    b. Symbolic Mode

    The most commonly used symbols to assign the permissions.

8. File Permissions

    a. Absolute Mode

        i. Command: $ chmod [-r] mode Filename

        ii. Modes:

            0   :   No Permission

            1   :   execute

            2   :   write

            4   :   read

    b. Symbolic Mode

        i. Command: $ chmod who opcode mode filename

        ii. who:

            u :   users

            g :   group

            o :   others

            a :   all (default)

        iii. opcode:

            + :   grant

            :   to revoke

            = :   to assign

        iv. mode:

            r :   read

            w :   write

            x :   execute

9. Change ownership

    a. Command for system that changes the owner of a file.

    b. Command:

        chown [-option] newowner filenames

        Note: Only superuser can change

10. Change Group

    For system changes the group that has access to a file or directory.

    a. Command: chgrp newgroup filenames

        Note: Only superuser can change the

        group.

Unit 7

Pipes and Filters

11. Pipe Command

    a. A pipe is a mechanism which takes the output of one command as the input for the next command.

    b. It is denoted by the symbol (|)

    c. Problems:

        i. Find how many users logged in ?

        ii. Display first two lines of red file. (use Pipe command)

12. Filters

    d. A filter takes input from the standard input, process it and then sends the output to the standard output. Filters also take input from a file.

    e. Types of Filters

        i. Sort Filter

        ii. Grep Filter

        iii. Egrep Filter

        iv. Fgrep Filter

        v. Uniq Filter

        vi. Pg Filter

        vii. More filter

13. Sort Filter

    f. Used for sorting

    g. The options are:

        i. Without option

        ii. -r

        iii. -n

        iv. +pos –pos option

            1. $sort +pos –pos

            filename Where

                +pos indicates total number of previous field

                -pos indicates position of field to be sorted

              Note : This option takes space as the delimiter between the fields

        v. -t option

            1. Used if delimiter between the fields are other than the space

      vi.   -u options

          1.   it allows unique record only and suppress the duplicate records

          2. $sort –ufiename

      vii. -o option

          1.   Instead of showing sorted files in the standard output (monitor) can be stored in thefile

          2. $sort –o fiename1 filename2

             Where

                 Filename1 – is the new file name

                 Filename2 – is the file to be sorted

Filter Commands

14. A filter takes input from the standard input, process it and then sends the output to the standard output. Filters also take input from a file.Types of filters are :

    a.   Grep Filters

    b.   Egrep Filters

    c.   Fgrep Filters

    d.   Uniq Filter

    e.   More Filter

    f.   Pg Filter

15. Grep Filter

    a.   Used to filter the records.

    b.   The options are:

        i.   -i

        ii. -n

        iii. -c

        iv. -v

    c.   Filtering by range([...])

        i. $ cat new

             this is a new file

             the files are

             newa, newb, newc

             which are good files

        ii. $ grep "new[a-b]" new

           Output: newa, newb, newc

   d. Filtering by ending letter($)

      i. Filter the records which end with 'e'

      ii. $ grep "e$" data

           Output : france 800   europe

   e. Filtering by Starting letter(^)

      i. Filter the records which start with 'n'

      ii. $ grep "^n" data

           Output : nigeria 750   Africa

16. Egrep Filter

   a. Grep filter can filter records by only one condition

   b. Egrep is a extended grep which we can filter through many conditions

      i. Filter the records which contains india, nigeria and france

         1. $ egrep "india|nigeria|france" data

         Output : india   200   asia

               nigeria 750   Africa

               france 800   europe

      ii. Filter the records which ends with "ica"

         1. $ egrep "(ica)$" data

         Output : nigeria 750   Africa

               maxiew 750   north america

      iii. Filter the records by giving the condition through file

         1. First create a file and write the conditions in it.

            a. $ cat>countries

                 france

                 india

            b. $ cat countries

                 france

                 India

         2. Attach the filename as condition by using –f option in egrep filter

    a. $ egrep -f countries

    data india   200

                 asia

    france 800   europe

17. Fgrep Filter

a. Fgrep is the fixed grep which is used to extract only fixed strings

   i. $ cat>old

     This   is   a

     teacher We are

     students This is

     a book

     We came here for studying

     this is a good practices

   ii. $ fgrep "This is" old

    This is a teacher

    This is a book

   iii. $ fgrep -i "This is" old

    This is a teacher

    This is a book

    this is a good practices

18. Uniq Filter

a. Learn through Help

19. Pg Filter

a. Page filter is used to display output of a command page by page

b. To move to next page, press enter key

c. For Example,

$ls –l|pg

20. More Filter

a. Similar to Page Filter

b. It is used to display output of a command page by page

c. To move to next page, press space bar key

d. For Example,

$ls –l|more

21. Cut Command

a. Use to cut the fields

b. If delimiter is other than space, use '-d' option

c. To cut the second field

    i. cat>mast

       red   yellow green

       blue   black orange

       purple violet indigo

    ii. $ cat mast

       red   yellow green

       blue   black orange

       purple violet indigo

    iii. $ cut -f2 mast

       yellow

       black

       Violet

d. To cut the second filed if delimter is ':'

    i. $ cat>trans

       hai:good:bad

       welcome:to:syscoms

    ii. $ cat trans

       hai:good:bad

       welcome:to:syscoms

    iii. $ cut -d":" -f2 trans

       good

       to

22. Paste Command

a. It is used to paste the content of the files

    i. $ cat data

       india 200   asia

       china 500   Asia

       nigeria 750   Africa

       maxiew 750   north america

       france 800   europe

    ii. $ cat mast

       red   yellow green

       blue   black orange

       purple violet indigo

    iii. $ paste data mast

       india 200   asia   red   yellow green

china   500   Asia   blue   black orange

nigeria 750   Africa purple violet indigo

maxiew 750   north america

france 800   europe

23. Tee Command

a. Used to store the output temporarily

b. For example

    i. $ cat trans|sort|tee temp|cut -d":" -f1

      hai

      welcome

    ii. $ cat temp

      hai:good:bad

      welcome:to:syscoms

24. Translate Command

a. Used to translate characters from one to other

b. For example,

    i. To Convert a file into upper case,

    ii. $ cat data|tr "[a-z]" "[A-Z]"

      INDIA   200   ASIA

      CHINA   500   ASIA

      NIGERIA 750   AFRICA

      MAXIEW 750   NORTH AMERICA

      FRANCE 800   EUROPE

Unit 8

Processing and Communication

1. Process

Two types of process

        a. Foreground process

        b. Background process

2. Foreground Process

A foreground job can receive keyboard input and signals from the controlling terminal

Foreground process are terminated by pressing **Ctrl z**

If the login session is disconnected, foreground jobs are terminated automatically

3. Background Process

A process which run at the background without any user intervention

To put a job at background, type an ampersand (&) at the end of the command

Background process will be killed when user logs out

Example for background process

$sort –o countrydata data &

Ls /dev/null|tee temp &

"[ ]" numbers are the job numbers

4.   Jobs command—Check the status of jobs in the current session

5.   bg command—Run the most recently stopped job in the background

6.   Fg command—Bring most recently background job to the foreground

fg %1—Bring a job to foreground by specifying its job number after the percent sign

7. Nohup command

Nohup(no hangup) command is used to execute the background process even after the user has logged out

For example,

$nohup sort red &

8.   Process Status (ps Command)

Ps command is used to display the attributes of a process and it is used to kill the process by identifying the process number

The options of ps commands

are: ps

ps –f

ps –f –u syscoms

ps –a

ps –e

ps –ae

ps -ge

9. Termination of a Process

You can terminate a process with the kill command.

Command:

$ kill -9 PID

$ kill -9 0 (to kill all process including Login shell

10. Setting Terminal Characteristics

The terminal is the device by which a user communicates with the system.

Command:

$ stty

How will you change the key combination to terminate the input stream?

11. Managing Disk Space

Linux has a number of commands like the df and du. These commands can also issued by any user.

Command:

 # df

$ df

Option:

-t

12. Disk Usage

To find out the consumption of a specified directory tree rather than an entire file system.

Command:

 # du

Options:

-s

13. Engaging a File System

The command which use to mount file system.

Command:

$ mount [option] *type device dir*

Disengaging a File System

Command use to remove the attachment of file system mounted on target.

Command:

$ unmount

14. File Types

Compressed / Archived Files

File Formats

System Files

Scripting Files

Compressed

Files

.z (a compressed file)

.tar   (an archive file)

.gz(an compressed file)

.tgz   (an tarred & gzipped files)

File Formats

.txt   (A plain ASCII text file)

.html/ .htm   (an HTML file)

.ps   (A postscript file)

.au   (An audio file)

.wav   (An audio file)

.xpm   (An image file)

.jpg   (An graphical or image file)

.gif   (An graphical or image file)

.pdf   (An electronic image file)

System Files

.rpm   (Red Hat Package Manager file)

.conf   (A configuration file)

.a   (an archive file)

.lock   (a "lock" file; determines whether a program is in use) Scripting

Files

.h   (A C or C++ program language header file)

.c   (a C program language source code file)

.cpp (A C++ program language source code file)

.o   (A program object file)

.pl   (A Perl script)

.so (A library file)

15. Backup of Directory to a Floppy

For taking a backup to a floppy we use the **tar** command.

Command:

$ tar –cvf /dev/fd0 *.doc

What is the precautionary step to be followed before backup?

<u>Communication</u>

16. The Universal Mailer

mail is the command which use to send and see a mail.

To send a mail,

$ mail username

To check the mail,

$mail

17. Broadcast a Message

Command "**wall**" is used to broadcast commands to all the users

Command:

$ wall

This command can be executed only by the user having administrator privilege

18. Message for User

To send message to a

user Command:

$ write username

$ hello username

Query?

What is the difference between hello and write command?

What will you do if your colleague is disturbing by sending the message?[hint : $mesg –n]

19. Command to select a printer

Command used to check the configured printer.

Command:

$ cat /etc/printcap

It will show the list of all configured printer in your terminal

20. Printing a File

Command used to print a file

Command:

$ lpr [options] [filename ...]

Eg: To print the garments.txt to selected printer "lp" given the following command:

$ lpr -P lp garments/garments.txt

Status of the printer

To find the status of the printer,

$lpstat

21. Canceling Print Command

To canceling the queued print job the command

Command:

$ lpq

$ lprm <job>

22. Tee Command

Accept output from another command and send it both to standard output and to *files* (like a T or fork in the road).

Command:

$ ls -l | tee savefile View listing and save for later

Unit 9

Editing the File

1. The VI Editor

> **VI** Editor is an editor which helps to edit any text file, like editing text, deleting text, moving cursor forward and backward etc.

2. Advantages of VI Editor

It does not consume an inordinate amount of system resources.

> Vi works great over slow network PPP modem connections and on systems of limited resources.

3. The Three Modes

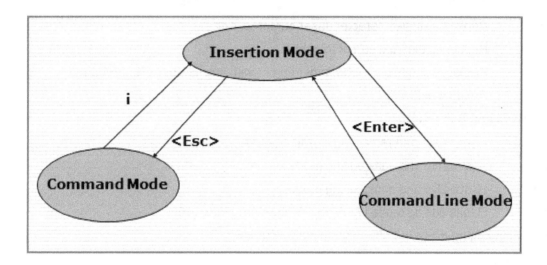

> **a. Insert Mode**

Text is inserted. The ESC key ends insert mode and returns you to command mode. One can enter insert mode with the "i" (insert), "a" (insert after), "A" (insert at end of line), "o" (open new line after current line) or "O" (Open line above current line) commands.

> **b. Command Mode**

Letters or sequence of letters interactively command vi. Commands are case sensitive. The ESC key can end a command.

> **c. Command Line Mode**

One enters this mode by typing ":" which puts the command line entry at the foot of the screen.

4. Cursor Movement

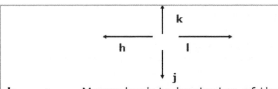

b : Moves back to beginning of the word

e : Moves forward to end of the word.

w : Moves forward to beginning of the word

5. Input Mode Command

i : Insert text to left of cursor.

I : Insert text at beginning of line.

a : Appends text to right of cursor.

A : Append text at end of line.

o : Open line below.

0 : open line above.

rch: Replaces single character unser cursor with ch.

R : Replaces text from cursor to right.

s : Replaces single character under cursor with any number of characters.

S : Replace entire line.

6. Save and Exit Command

:w : Saves file and remaining in editing mode.

:x : Saves file and quits editing mode.

:wq : Saves file and quits editing mode.

:q : Quits editing mode when no changes are made to file.

:q! : Quits editing mode but after abandoning changes.

:sh : Escape to Linux shell command.

7. Paging and scrolling

<ctrl-f> : Scrolls full page forward.

<ctrl-b> : Scrolls full page backward.

<ctrl-d> : Scrolls half page forward.

<ctrl-u> : Scrolls half page backward.

<ctrl-l> : Redraws the screen.

8. Deletion

The simplest text deletion is achieved with the **x** command. This command deletes the character under the cursor.

Command:

x   # Deletes a single character.

The simplest line deletion is achieved with the **dd** command. This command deletes the entire line under the cursor.

Command: dd

Exercise

Type the following program to get practice in the VI Editor. The below program is for just typing and not for compilation or execution.

$ vi first

```
public class Student{ private
    String name; private int
    id; private double gpa;

    public Student(int id, String name, double gpa){ this.id = id;
        this.name = name; this.gpa
        = gpa;
    }

    public Student(int id, double gpa){ this(id, "", gpa);
    }

    public String getName(){ return
        name;
    }
    public int getId() { return id;
    }
    public double getGPA(){ return
        gpa;
    }

    public void setName(String newName){ this.name =
        newName;
    }
    public String toString(){
        return "Student:\nID: "+id+"\nName: "+name+"\nGPA:"+gpa;
    }
}
```

Unit 10

Shell programming Basics

1. Variables

Variable is a temporary storage to store a date

For example, a=10

To print the value of the variable: echo $a

To input the value for variable: read a

2. Operators

      a. Assignment operator

         =(Equal to)

      b. Arithmetic Operators

         +, -, *, /

      c. Relational Operators

         le (lesser than or equal

         to) lt (Lesser than)

         ge (Greater than or equal

         to) gt (Greater than)

         eq (Equal to)

         ne (Not Equal to)

      d. Logical Operators

         a (And)

         o (Or)

3. Expression

Expression is a statement containing both operator and
operands. In unix , expression is written as

    C = `expr $a \* 5`

4. Types of Programming

      a. Sequential – Executed line by line

      b. Conditional – Executed based on the condition

      c. Repetitive or Iterative – Executed repeatedly

Examples for Sequential Statement

=======================

$vi seqst

program for area of rectangle

Echo "Enter length"

Read l

Echo "Enter Breadth"

Read b

Area = `expr $l \* $b`

Echo "The area of rectangle is $area"

$sh seqst

Conditional Statements

==================

If statement

if [cond]

then

statement

fi

If ..then…else statement

If [condition]

then

Statement1

Elif

Statement2

Elif

Statement3

.

.

Else

Statement.

fi

Example for if…then…else statement

========================

program to find greatest of 2 numbers

Echo "Enter first number"

Read a

Echo "Enter second number"

Read b

If [$a –gt $b]

Then

Echo "First number is greater"

Else

Echo "Second number is greater"

Fi

program to find the greatest of three numbers

Echo "Enter first number"

Read a

Echo "Enter second number"

Read b

Echo "Enter third number"

Read c

If [$a –gt $b –a $a –gt $c]

Then

Echo "a is greater"

Elif [$b –gt $c]

Then

Echo "b is greater"

Else

Echo "C is greater"

Fi

Case Statement

===========

Used as an alternative of if…then else statement

Case $variable in

statement1;;

2)statement2;;

.

.

*) Statement;;

esac

Program to input number from 1 to 3 and print it in letter form

Echo "Enter the number"

Read n

Case $n in

Echo '"one";;

Echo "two";;

Echo "three";;
*) Echo "Invalid No";;
Esac

Repetitive Statement
===============
In repetitive statement following attribute should be present
1. Initial value
2. Final value
3. Either Increment or Decrement value

Types of repetitive statement
1. While loop statement
2. Until loop statement
3. For loop statement

While loop statement
====================

While [cond]
do
statement
done

In while statement if condition is true, it will go for looping and when condition become false it exit the while statement
# program to print a number from 1 to 5
i=1
while [$i –le 5]
do
Echo $n
i = `expr $i + 1`
done

Until loop statement

================

Until [cond]

do

statement

done

In until statement if condition is false, it will go for looping and when condition become true it exit the while statement. It is the reverse of while loop statement

program to print a number from 1 to 5

i=1

until [$i –ge 5]

do

echo $n

i = `expr $i + 1`

done

For loop statement

==============

for $variable in <value>

do

statement

done

program to print a number from 1 to 5

For $i in 1 2 3 4 5

do

echo $i

done

For loop statement is not successful because suppose if you want to print a number from 1 to 100,you have to mention all the numbers in the for loop program.

Problem

1.   Write a shell script to display the following details in a pay slip:

Pay Slip Details

1.HRA

2.DA

3.PF

HRA is calculated as 20% of basic, DA as 40% of basic and PF as 10% of basic

Command Line Arguments

Command line arguments are the arguments passed while executing a

file For examaple,

$sh filename arg1,arg2,arg3

Test on file Types

==============

-f To check for existence of the ordinary file

-d To check for the existence of directory

-r File Readable

-w File Writable

-x File Executable

-s File exists and if it is not empty

2.   Write a shell program to accept the file or directory as command line argument and check for file or directory.

```
$vi filecheck
If [ $# -lt 1 ]
Then
Echo "File is not passed as a
argument" Exit
Fi
If [ -f $1 ]
Then
Echo "$1 is an ordinary file"
Elif [-d $1]
Then
Echo "$1 is a directory"
Else
Echo "$1 does not exist"
Fi
$sh filecheck red
```

Model Exam for UNIX Commands

1. Create a file called "test" with the following contents: (use **cat**)
   Note that the second test did not go to work at all since an error was reported while executing the first test.

2. How would you perform the following operations: [2.3]
   a) Create 3 empty files empty1, empty2, empty3

   b) Create a file called "text" and store your Name, Course name, UOH ID and Address in it.

   c) Display the contents of the file text on the screen.

   d) Make a copy of the file text into another file newtext

   e) Create a file matter and type any two sentences in it.

   f) Combine the contents of the file text and matter into another file txtmat.

   g) Delete the file text.

   h) Create one more link called tmpfile for the file matter

   i) Change the permissions for the file newtext to 600.

   j) Rename the file newtext to oldtext.

   k) Create a directory mydir in the current directory.

   l) Move the files oldtext and matter to the directory mydir.

3. Create a file called "test" with the following contents: (use **cat**)
   10 ali 900 saudi
   80 mamdoah 600 mexico
   56 Fatima 550 tasmania
   78 Naif 600 australia
4. Sort the test file in the reverse order and save it in a file called "reverse"
5. Sort the reverse file based on 2nd field.
6. Retrieve the records which contains 600 in the file "reverse" with the line number
7. Retrieve the records with ends with "ia"
8. Retrieve the records which contains the string "56 Fatima"
9. Display only the last 3 lines of test file.
10. Display from the 3rd record of the test file.
11. Display the number of words, characters and lines in the test file
12. Calculate 4*3-3/2 it should display in one decimal
13. The more filter display the output page by page by pressing_key
14. Cut the second field in the test file.
15. Grant execute permission for other user in test file and check the permission
16. Convert all the data in test file to upper case.

Model Exam for Shell programming

Sphere

<u>Surface
Area</u>

$A = 4 \pi r^2$

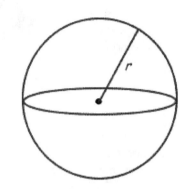

<u>Volume</u>

$V = \frac{4}{3} \pi r^3$

Write a shell programming to perform the following output:
****
MATHEMATICAL
CALCULATION
****

1.Volume of sphere
2.Printing the number in
reverse ENTER YOUR
CHOICE:
1
Enter the
radius 3
 Volume of sphere is : 81
Do you want to continue(1-yes, 2- No)? 1

****
MATHEMATICAL
CALCULATION
****

1.Volume of sphere
2.Printing the number in
reverse ENTER YOUR
CHOICE:
2
Enter the
number 482
Reverse : 284
Do you want to continue(1-yes, 2- No)? 2

Authors' Profile

Dr. Mohammed Fakrudeen is experienced in design and development of core infrastructure systems, and in management of a team and projects. He has extensive background in Web accessibility including experience in evaluating web sites for accessibility feature, analyzing impact of ICT for blind deaf and Cognitive Disabilities, developing personal Learning Environment for special Education by using cloud computing; he has prepared and supported the software for Order Management System, License Management System by using Oracle Apps. He is a well experienced trainer for practical in management of Windows and Unix/Linux; in programming using Basic, Pascal, Lisp, Scheme, ML, Prolog, Smalltalk, Assembler x86; in applications of many software packages including Microsoft Office, WordPerfect Suite, LaTeX, Paradox, Btrieve, Mathematica. He has published numerous research papers in journals and conference proceedings. He has completed Ph.D. in Computer Science from Anglia Ruskin University, United Kingdom.

Dr. Shahanawaj Ahamad is an active academician and researcher in the field of Computer Science and Software Engineering, working as Assistant Professor, Chairperson of Software Engineering Research, Program Coordinator of Software Engineering, Dy. Director of Quality Assurance & Development and Chairperson of Dept. Graduate Curriculum Development in College of Computer Science & Engineering, University of Ha'il, K.S.A. He is member of ACM, British Computer Society, Computer Society of India, IAENG with membership of various national and international academic and research organizations. He is currently working on SOA, Software Aging and Evolution, published more than thirty research articles in national and international journals and conference proceedings. He holds M.Tech. followed by Ph.D. in Computer Science with specialization in Software Engineering from Jamia Millia Islamia Central University, New Delhi, India. He has supervised bachelor senior projects, COOP training, master and Ph.D. dissertations.

www.ingramcontent.com/pod-product-compliance
Lightning Source LLC
Chambersburg PA
CBHW060504060326
40689CB00020B/4626